This Fabulous Century 1920-1930

This booklet has been adapted and produced especially for TIME Magazine by TIME-LIFE BOOKS from the series This Fabulous Century.

Contents

© 1988 TIME-LIFE BOOKS INC.
First printing 1988. Printed in U.S.A.
Published simultaneously in Canada.

America
1920-1930

Fifth Avenue at 42nd Street, New York, 1926.

An Age of Sheiks and Shebas

They're all desperadoes, these kids, all of them with any life in their veins; the girls as well as the boys; maybe more than the boys.

FLAMING YOUTH BY WARNER FABIAN

The '20s were an exciting—and perhaps a frightening—time to be young. It was the era of the First Youth Rebellion. Once boys had tried to be paragons of gallantry, industry and idealism; girls had aspired to seem modest and maidenly. Now all that had changed. "The uncertainties of 1919 were over," F. Scott Fitzgerald wrote. "America was going on the greatest, gaudiest spree in history."

In a refrain that would be heard again and again in later generations, John F. Carter Jr. wrote in the *Atlantic Monthly:* "I would like to observe that the older generation had certainly pretty well ruined this world before passing it on to us. They give us this Thing, knocked to pieces, leaky, red-hot, threatening to blow up; and then they are surprised that we don't accept it with the same enthusiasm with which they received it."

The new questioning of their elders' authority, combined with the relative affluence of the decade, spawned a breed of youngsters who claimed to be hard-boiled, heavy-drinking and daring—and sometimes were. The girls in particular seemed to have changed. Skirts were shorter than ever before. Cloche hats, silk stockings, fake jewelry, bobbed hair replaced the osprey plumes, hobble skirts and flowing tresses of yesteryear. The advent of Pro-

hibition made clandestine drinking an appealing game; women took up the sport alongside men. They also took up smoking; sales of cigarettes doubled during the decade.

Morals were undergoing a revolution. More and more college-age boys owned automobiles—and were parking them on dark roads to "neck" with their dates. Suddenly Freud's name was on everyone's lips. One writer complained: "Today, let some ingenue venture, 'I had the queerest dream—' and all at once we see a crowd, a host of parlor analysts. The obliging interpreters listen,—though this is hardly necessary,—look wise, and at the end exclaim 'Aha! That means *sex!* You have a sex-complex!' "

Inevitably, the daring clothes, the scandalous dances and sensual jazz, the late-night parties and cynical opinions of the youth drew the wrath of many members of the older generation. "The situation," declared a Southern Baptist publication, "causes grave concern on the part of all who have the ideals at heart of purity and home life and the stability of our American civilization."

But America's young people didn't care. They went right on in their heedless, happy way, adopting the outrageous fashions shown on the following pages, and singing, "In the mean time, in between time, ain't we got fun?"

Poised and chic, the epitome of the sophisticated flapper, Suzette Dewey, daughter of the Assistant Secretary of the Treasury, steps out of her roadster.

Two young ladies display the latest in winter wear: open galoshes and cloche hats.

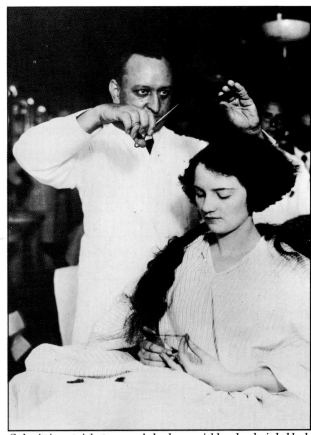

Submitting stoicly to a men's barber, a girl has her hair bobbed.

An amateur artist decorates a flapper's full-length rain slicker.

Comic Joe E. Lewis displays patterned golf hose, baggy knickers and bow tie.

Patent-leather hair, center-parted, provides the movie-hero look.

A young man in Los Angeles proudly shows off his flappy white "Oxford bags."

Garbed in a raccoon coat and peekaboo hat, a lady of fashion enters her auto.

A girl in a short skirt and turned-down hose powders her knees.

A Suddenly Smaller World

The airplane has now advanced to the stage where the demands of commerce are sufficient to warrant the building of planes without regard to military usefulness. Undoubtedly in a few years the United States will be covered with a network of passenger, mail and express lines. CHARLES A. LINDBERGH, *WE,* 1927

For American airmen, the early 1920s were years of frustration. During the war, many of them had known adulation; in particular, the folks back home had avidly followed the exploits of the pursuit pilots, whose man-to-man dogfights had supplied a touch of personal combat amid the mechanized slaughter of trench warfare. Now, most Americans had reverted to their old conviction that if God had wanted men to fly, He would have given them wings. Some fliers turned to other ways of making a living: Eddie Rickenbacker, America's Ace of Aces, sold autos. But there was a small group of men who doggedly stuck to the air; they soon found themselves engaged in a strange variety of airborne activities.

Ben O. Howard, pilot turned airplane designer, found a lucrative market in building planes for bootleggers, who needed the aircraft to smuggle illegal liquor across the Canadian or Mexican borders. Howard also flew the contraband cargoes himself—and got used to being shot at by moonshiners who thought they were being hunted from the air by revenue agents. Famed instructor and pilot Casey Jones sped urgent news photos cross-country. Another pilot, Roscoe Turner, set up an airline that ran from Los Angeles to Reno, renowned for quickie divorces; Tur-

ner's route became known as the "Alimony Special." After this venture folded, Turner convinced an oil company whose trademark was a lion that it could get enormous publicity if it hired him to fly around the country with a lion cub as his passenger. The lion liked to fly, but the Humane Society insisted that Turner strap a parachute on the beast. Luckily, the cub never had to jump.

That was more than could be said about the pilots who worked for the Post Office Department's infant air-mail service. Flying without instruments in all kinds of weather, many of them died when their planes iced up or hit mountainsides, but a good number were saved by their 'chutes. A tall, slender young air-mail pilot named Charles A. Lindbergh bailed out four times without ever losing faith in aviation. In 1927 Lindbergh took off from Roosevelt Field, Long Island, in a tiny plane, and headed out over the ocean, bound for Europe. Some 33.5 hours later he landed in Paris—and was stunned by the hysterical acclaim that greeted him. It was a justified tribute, for Lindbergh's exploit, the first nonstop solo transatlantic flight, was the transcendentally dramatic event which proved that the age of air transportation had truly begun. With this flight, the world was suddenly smaller.

Lindbergh stands beside "The Spirit of St. Louis." He identified himself with his plane so closely that he used the term "we" in telling of their flight.

All That Jazz

Carroll Dickerson's band plays for a jazz floor show: Chicago, 1924.

A modest canopy advertises Barron's Cabaret, a Harlem joint where jazz flourished. Duke Ellington got his start here in 1923.

Louis Armstrong in the mid-'20s: boiled shirt, shy grin and gleaming trumpet, the brilliantly toned horn he had exchanged for the cornet.

An elegant George Gershwin puffs a cigar and makes musical notations in a 1927 portrait by the great photographer Edward Steichen.

Matchless Melodies and "Symphonic" Jazz

Perhaps the most celebrated musical event of the decade was the premier of George Gershwin's *Rhapsody in Blue* at Manhattan's Aeolian Hall in the winter of 1924. Many of New York's bluest blue bloods and all of its music critics practically stormed the old concert hall. Paul Whiteman, the chubby bandleader who conducted the *Rhapsody,* went out front before the concert started and saw a mob scene. "Men and women were fighting to get into the door," Whiteman reported, "pulling and mauling each other as they sometimes do at a baseball game, or a prize fight, or in the subway." The furor outlasted the concert; the critics either praised the music or damned it unmercifully. Deems Taylor, considered the dean of the critics, was for it. He found that the *Rhapsody* revealed "a genuine melodic gift and a piquant and individual harmonic sense." Taylor added, "Moreover, it is genuine jazz music."

It wasn't at all, of course—"symphonic jazz" perhaps, but not the real article. Nevertheless, though Gershwin didn't write jazz, he was the beau ideal of the Jazz Age. He was handsome, forceful, independent and charming —and he became quite rich. Above all he was spectacularly successful in an era that worshipped success. It was not quite rags to riches, although people often said it was. His parents were Russian immigrants, but Morris Gershovitz—that was the real family name—always had enough money for food, and even piano lessons. Nevertheless George had moved from a boyhood on the Lower East Side to the best salons of New York and London, where he hobnobbed with millionaires, duchesses and other celebrities of the time. And he was an undoubted genius at writing the show tunes that everybody whistled and hummed. Not just show tunes but whole shows full of them. And marvelous ones. They were original, fresh, clever, timely, and often quite beautiful—"Lady Be Good," "I've Got a Crush on You," "The Man I Love," "Someone to Watch Over Me," "Looking for a Boy" . . . the list could go on and on.

These tunes were not jazz (jazz was a way of performing music, rather than a way of writing it); but, ironically, many quickly became "jazz standards"—that is, tunes jazzmen loved to play and improvise around. Another irony of Gershwin's relationship with jazz is that he himself adored the music. As a boy of eight he would roller skate through Harlem to 134th Street and sit on the curb outside Barron D. Wilkins' club and listen to that proto-jazz called ragtime float out the door. The first song on which he collaborated with his lyric-writing brother Ira proclaimed that "the great American folk song is a rag." His own piano playing had a very jazzy touch—angular, swift, offbeat. But he couldn't write the stuff, as the bemused critics and public thought. He was just a great song writer, possibly the best that ever lived.

If Americans adored George Gershwin, they went absolutely (and inexplicably) mad for Paul Whiteman and his orchestra. A young violinist from Denver, Colorado, Whiteman came East in 1920 and was soon acclaimed the King of Jazz—or sometimes the Prince, as in this ditty published in *Vanity Fair:*

> *J is for JAZZ by our plump Prince of Whales*
> *Whiteman, who staggers the musical scales.*

By 1922 he could command $25,000 for a six-night engagement, an enormous sum at the time and one that was unmatched for decades. When he married a dancer named Vanda Hoff it was front-page news. When he went on a diet and managed to lose 100 pounds—normally his face and figure resembled comedian Oliver Hardy's—two books were written about his ordeal. When he went to Europe he was so lavishly entertained that he gained 40 pounds back. On his return he was honored with a reception at the Waldorf-Astoria. The reason for this adulation is hard to imagine. Whiteman frequently had a topflight musician or two in his band (Bix Beiderbecke was one who played for him), but otherwise it was a mediocre outfit that burbled along without much beat, tone or imagination. Its popularity was, in short, a fad, an aberration of the dizzy decade. But there was nothing ephemeral about the real jazz, the glorious crazy-quilt of sound that spilled out of Barron Wilkins' and a thousand other joints to add the spice of originality to American music.

Panic roils Wall Street on October 24, 1929.

Boom and Bust

Business Fever

We have had booms and collapses in the past. But now we have no boom. Our pro-
gress is rapid—but sure. Buying is now larger than it ever was—but it is not frenzied.
The kind of emotion which brings on a boom is absent.

SAMUEL CROWTHER IN *COLLIER'S*, 1926

When President Coolidge declared in 1925 that "The business of America is business," he was putting it mildly —and belatedly. Three full years had passed since the end of the postwar recession, and business had become a national obsession. Everyone was spending avidly and the economy was spiraling upward at a record clip.

Production was up. The torrential output of consumer goods included such desirable new products as radios and electric refrigerators, along with countless improved models of standard items—faster cars, shinier bathroom fixtures, even plusher caskets. Competition for sales was healthily stiff—and getting stiffer all the time.

Corporate profits were up. Thanks to new techniques of mass production, many manufacturers netted huge sums that they liberally plowed back into plant expansion. In 1923 U.S. Steel was operating so efficiently that it was able to reduce its workday from twelve to eight hours, to employ 17,000 additional workers, to raise wages and yet, amazingly, to show an increase in profits.

Income was up in most lines of endeavor. Even the industrial workers, whose strikes for higher pay had availed them little in the previous decade, benefited from company largesse and enjoyed a higher standard of living. To round out the happy picture, prices were stable; savings and life insurance doubled; and business was given added impetus by the growth of chain stores and installment buying. With all these factors reinforcing the upward spiral, prosperity seemed to have no ceiling.

In the full flush of fiscal euphoria, the country brought its swollen profits and abundant credit to bear in wild get-rich-quick speculation. By 1928 the prices of stocks had soared beyond the point of safe return as thousands of "little" people braved the hectic market seeking a share in overnight windfalls. A nurse made $30,000, a broker's valet amassed the tidy sum of a quarter-million.

At no time in the '20s were more than 1.5 million Americans involved in the market, but their much publicized successes fueled the reckless optimism of the country at large. Business, most people came to believe, would provide everyone with a steadily increasing share of ever-expanding prosperity. It now seemed almost unpatriotic to exercise restraint in buying. It seemed heretical to pay any heed to the likes of economist Roger Babson, when he warned: "Sooner or later a crash is coming, and it may be terrific." America was a nation of giddy consumers for whom wishful thinking had become a way of life.

A 1921 cartoon entitled "The Anglers" shows shady operators fishing for victims in the stock exchange—a graphic warning widely ignored.

Collapse and Confusion on the Market

In November 1929, soon after the stock market crash, a New York policeman found a bedraggled parrot. In a fitting epitaph to the disaster, the bird kept squawking, "More margin! More margin!"

The lack of more margin was the straw that broke the back of the Big Bull Market and signaled the end of the Coolidge-Hoover prosperity. Before the market cracked, stocks were not only priced far above their real value; they were being bought for a marginal down payment of as little as 10 per cent, with the bulk of the purchase price financed by brokers' loans. As stock prices slumped, overextended investors were required to put up additional margin, and many could produce the capital only by selling off shares at distress prices. This drove the market into a steeper, broader descent—and redoubled the brokers' demands for margin. Between late October and mid-November, stocks lost more than 40 per cent of their total valuation—a drop of $30 billion in paper values.

Those few weeks were a nightmare. Market-wise reporters struggled in vain to describe adequately the pandemonium on the stock exchange floor. Broker Fred Schwed later wrote ironically: "Like all life's rich emotional experiences, the full flavor of losing important money cannot be conveyed by literature." Only slowly, as personal anecdotes fleshed out the appalling statistics, did the scope of the Crash become amply evident.

One woman, presented by her broker with an enormous bill for more margin, cried out in bewilderment, "How could I lose $100,000? I never *had* $100,000." Facing the mad scramble to obtain margin money, pawnbrokers had to turn away hundreds seeking loans on jewelry.

October 29, when stocks suffered their worst losses *(opposite)*, was catastrophic for almost everyone but a shrewd (and possibly apocryphal) messenger boy. Noting that a big block of White Sewing Machine stock was being offered at any price with no takers, he allegedly snapped it up at a dollar a share.

In an effort to bolster confidence, John D. Rockefeller announced, "My son and I have for some days been purchasing sound common stocks." A spirited rejoinder came from one of many hard-hit celebrities, comedian Eddie Cantor: "Sure, who else had any money left?"

The president of Union Cigar, stunned when his company's stock plummeted from $113.50 to four dollars in a day, fell or jumped to his death from the ledge of a New York hotel. Tales of suicide became standard fare in the mythology of the Crash. Actually, the suicide rate was higher in the few months before the Crash than in those just after it. Still, thousands of people had lost everything but their lives, and there was much truth to one man's remark that, while Jerusalem had only one Wailing Wall, "in Wall Street every wall is wet with tears."

In the aftermath, the country seemed to pause with bated breath while its leaders formed opinions. Their confident verdicts were not long in coming. Said President Hoover: "The fundamental business of the country, that is, production and distribution of commodities, is on a sound and prosperous basis." Statements by economists and businessmen pronounced stock prices "stabilized," the Crash "wholesome," the outlook "favorable."

But certain conditions, visible for months to anyone who put aside his rose-colored glasses, told quite another story: the economy was basically unsound. Banks and corporations were structurally weak and in many cases undermined by skullduggery and fraud. America's trade policies were self-defeating. The market for consumer goods was both glutted and untapped: 90 per cent of the nation's wealth was concentrated in the hands of only 13 per cent of the people; meanwhile, large depressed segments of society—among them farmers, textile workers and coal miners—lacked sufficient income to buy much more than their minimal needs. In its relation to these and other unhealthy symptoms, the stock market crash was far more than a private retribution for greedy speculators. It was a clear warning for all.

Yet most of the pundits held that prospects were bright, and everyone wanted to believe the good word. Tentatively reassured, people resumed their business pursuits, tried to recapture their boom-time zest for getting and spending. But somehow things were not quite the same.

PLUNGE OF A MARKET

1929. High.	1929. Low.	Stock and Dividend Rate.	First.	High.	Low.	Last.	Net Ch'ge.
57⅞	38	Abitibi Power & Paper.	40	40	38	38	— 6¼
112½	106	Abraham & S. pf. (7)*	107¼	107¼	107¼	107¼	— 2¾
96	84¾	Adams Express pf. (5)	87⅛	87⅛	87⅛	87⅛	+ ⅛
35⅞	24¾	Adams Millis (2)	26	26	24¾	24¾	— 2¾
104⅞	73	Advance Rumely	8¼	8¼	7	7	— 6¾
119	15	Advance Rumely pf....	20	20	15	16	— 7
4⅞	¾	Ahumada Lead	1	1	¾	¾	— ⅜
223⅜	95⅛	Air Reduction (†4½)...	125⅛	128	100¼	120	—25
48⅞	25	Air Way El. Appl. (2½)	25	25	25	25	— 3½
11¼	2½	Ajax Rubber	2½	2½	2½	2½	— ¼
10¼	4½	Alaska Juneau	5¼	5⅞	5	5⅞	..
25	5	Albany Perf. W. Paper	5	7	5	7	— 1
56½	18⅛	Alleghany Corporation.	24¼	24¾	18⅛	20⅝	— 8½
92	80⅛	Alleg. Corp. pf., x w. (5½)	88⅝	88⅝	88½	88½	— 1¼
354¾	204¾	Allied Chem. & Dye (6)	205	218	204¾	210	—35
125	120¼	Allied Chem. & D. pf. (7)	122	122	121	121	— ¼
75½	37¼	Allis-Chalmers Mfg. (2)	46½	47½	37¼	41	— 5
30½	29	Alpha Port. Cement (3)	30	30	30	30	— ¼
11⅛	3⅞	Amalgamated Leather.	3⅞	3⅞	3⅞	3⅞	— ⅜
42⅝	17½	Amerada Corp. (2)	20¼	21	17½	17½	— 4
23⅝	4	Am. Agricult. Chemical	7¼	7⅞	4	4	— 3⅝
73¾	25½	Am. Agricult. Chem. pf.	26	28½	25½	25½	— 5¾
60¼	46	Am. Beet Sugar pf....	49	49	49	49	..
76½	30	Am. Bosch Magneto ..	30	30	30	30	— 5
62	44½	Am. Br. S. & F. (2.40)	49	49½	44½	44½	— 5½
34¾	4⅛	Am. Brown Bov. Elec.	4¼	5½	4⅛	4⅛	— 6⅞
104	49¾	Am. Br. Bov. E. pf. (7)*	64	64	64	64	— 1
184½	107¾	Am. Can (†5)	130¼	134	110	120	—16
142	136½	Am. Can pf. (7)	136⅞	136⅞	136⅞	136⅞	— 1⅜
106½	76	Am. Car & Fdy. (6)...	81⅛	87½	76	87	+ 6⅞
120	110½	Am. Car & Fdy. pf. (7)	113	113	113	113	..
81⅝	35	Am. Chicle (2)	38½	38½	35	35	— 9
55	20	Am. Com. Alco. (k1.60)	20	30	20	30	— ¾
199¼	50	Am. & Foreign Power.	68	73	50	55	—22½
108½	104	Am. & F. Pwr. pf. (7)	106½	106½	106	106	— 1
103	87	Am. & F. Pw. 2d pf. (7)	89½	90	87	90	— 2½
42	21½	Am. Hawaiian S. S. (1)	21½	21½	21½	21½	— 1½
10	5	Am. Hide & Leather...	5	5	5	5	— 1
52¼	30¼	Am. Hide & Leath. pf.	32⅞	32⅞	31	31	— 4¼
85⅝	43½	Am. Home Prod. (3.60)	46¼	49	43½	47	— 3
54	30	Am. Ice (3)	33	35	30	35	— 2½
96	89¾	Am. Ice pf. (6)	90	90	90	90	..
96¾	30	Am. International (‡2).	30	41½	30	41½	— 2½
8⅞	2½	Am. La F. & Foamite..	3	3	2½	2½	— ⅞
136	99	Am. Locomotive (8) ...	101	101½	99	100	— ½
119⅞	112	Am. Locomotive pf. (7)	115	115¼	115	115	— ¾
279¾	147¼	Am. Mach. & Fdy. (†5)	185	185	175¼	175¼	—25¾
81¾	41⅛	Am. Metal (3)	41⅛	46	41⅛	46	— 7
98¼	65	Am. Nat. Gas pf. (7)*	78¼	78¼	78¼	78¼	— 1¾
17⅞	3½	Am. Piano	4	4	3½	3½	— 1½
55	18	Am. Piano pf. ....*	19	19	18	18	— 1
175¾	73¾	Am. Pwr. & Lgt. (¶1).	75¼	76¼	73¾	73¾	— 5¼
104	92¼	Am. P. & L. pf. (6)..	98⅛	98⅛	92¼	92¼	— 5¾
84¾	78	Am. P.&L. pf., A, sta. (5)	82⅛	82¼	80	80	— 2
55⅜	28	Am. Rad.&Sd. San. (1½)	30	32	29	32	+ 4
64¾	15	Am. Republics	15	20⅛	15	17⅞	— 4¼
144⅝	72	Am. Rolling Mill (c2)..	85⅛	89¾	72	72	—13
74¾	52	Am. Safety Razor (†5).	56⅞	56⅞	52	53¾	— 4¼
41⅞	29½	Am. Seating (2)	30	30	29½	29½	— ½
7	⅜	Am. Ship & Commerce.	1	1	⅝	⅝	— 1¾
112⅛	70	Am. Shipbuilding (8)..*	70	78	70	70	—10
130¼	81	Am. Smelt. & Ref. (4).	81	84¾	81	84	— 6
49	39	Am. Snuff (3)	40⅛	40½	39	39	— 2
79⅞	35¾	Am. Steel Found. (3)...	42½	43	35¾	40	— 5¼
114	110	Am. Stl. Found. pf. (7)*	111	111	110½	110½	— ½
85	40	Am. Stores (2½)	45	47	40	47	—13
94¾	66	Am. Sugar Refining (5)	70	70	66	66	— 6¾
111	102	Am. Sugar Ref. pf. (7).	103⅞	103⅞	102	103⅞	— ⅛
60	28	Am. Sumatra Tob. (3)..	32	33	28	29¾	— 3¼
310¼	193¼	Am. Tel. & Tel. (9)....	225	230	204	204	—28
232½	160	Am. Tobacco (8)	190	194½	182	191	— 5
235	160	Am. Tobacco, B (8)....	190	194¾	182	186	— 9¼
121¼	115	Am. Tobacco pf. (6)....	117	117	117	117	— 1
112	107¼	Am. Type Fdrs. pf. (7)*	109	109	108½	108½	— 1½
199	65	Am. Water Works (c1).	70	71	65	68	—12
104	97	Am. Wat. W. 1st pf. (6)	102⅝	102⅝	102⅝	102⅝	— ⅜
27⅞	5⅞	Am. Woolen	10⅛	10⅛	8	8⅛	— 3
58⅝	24	Am. Woolen pf.	25⅛	26	24	26	— 2⅛
46	37½	Am. Writ. Paper pf. (3)	37½	37½	37½	37½	— 1½
49¼	8⅛	Am. Zinc, L. & S.	8⅛	8⅛	8⅛	8⅛	— 2⅞
140	75½	Anaconda Copper (7)..	82	90½	75½	85	— 8½
80	25	Anchor Cap (2.40)......	40	40	25	35	—16
154½	102½	Anchor Cap pf. (6½)...	111	111	111	111	— 1
68⅜	30	Andes Copper (3)	34	38½	30	35	— 5¼
49½	22¾	Archer-Dan.-M. (2).....	30	31	22¾	24½	— 5¾
115	102¾	Archer-Dan.-M. pf. (7)*	104¼	104¼	104¼	104¼	— ¼
95	75	Armour of Del. pf. (7).	82¾	82¾	75	75	— 8
18⅜	5⅛	Armour of Ill., A......	5⅞	5⅞	5⅛	5⅞	— 1⅛
10¼	3½	Armour of Ill., B	3½	3⅞	3½	3½	— ⅝
40⅞	12	Arnold, Constable & Co.	12¼	13	12	12⅛	— 3¼
30	19⅝	Artloom (2)	22	22	22	22	— 1
30⅞	25	Art Metal Constr. (1½)	25½	26½	25	26½	+ 1⅜
58¾	35	Assoc. App. Ind. (4) ...	40	42	35	37	— 6
70¾	28	Assoc. D. G. (2½)	28	28	28	28	— 9¼
107	88¼	Assoc. D. G. 1st pf. (6)	91	93	91	93	+ ½
47¼	40½	Assoc. Oil (2) ....*	43¾	43¾	43¾	43¾	— ¾
298⅝	195⅛	At., T. & S. Fe (10)....	242½	244	221	234	—17
104¼	99	At., T. & S. Fe pf. (5).	102⅞	102⅞	101⅝	101⅝	— 1½
209½	165	Atl. Coast Line (†10)...	169½	169½	165	165	— 7
86⅞	32⅛	Atl., G. & W. I.	70	70⅞	67	67½	— 4⅜
62⅞	45¾	Atl., G. & W. I. pf. (4).	54¾	54¾	54½	54½	— ½
77⅞	30	Atl. Refining (†2)	30	38¾	30	35	— 5⅝
140	80	Atlas Powder (4)	91¼	93½	80	80	— 5
106½	98½	Atlas Powder pf. (6)..*	100	100	99	99	— 4
514	120	Auburn Auto (j4)	130	175	120	130	—60

PROFILE OF A STOCK

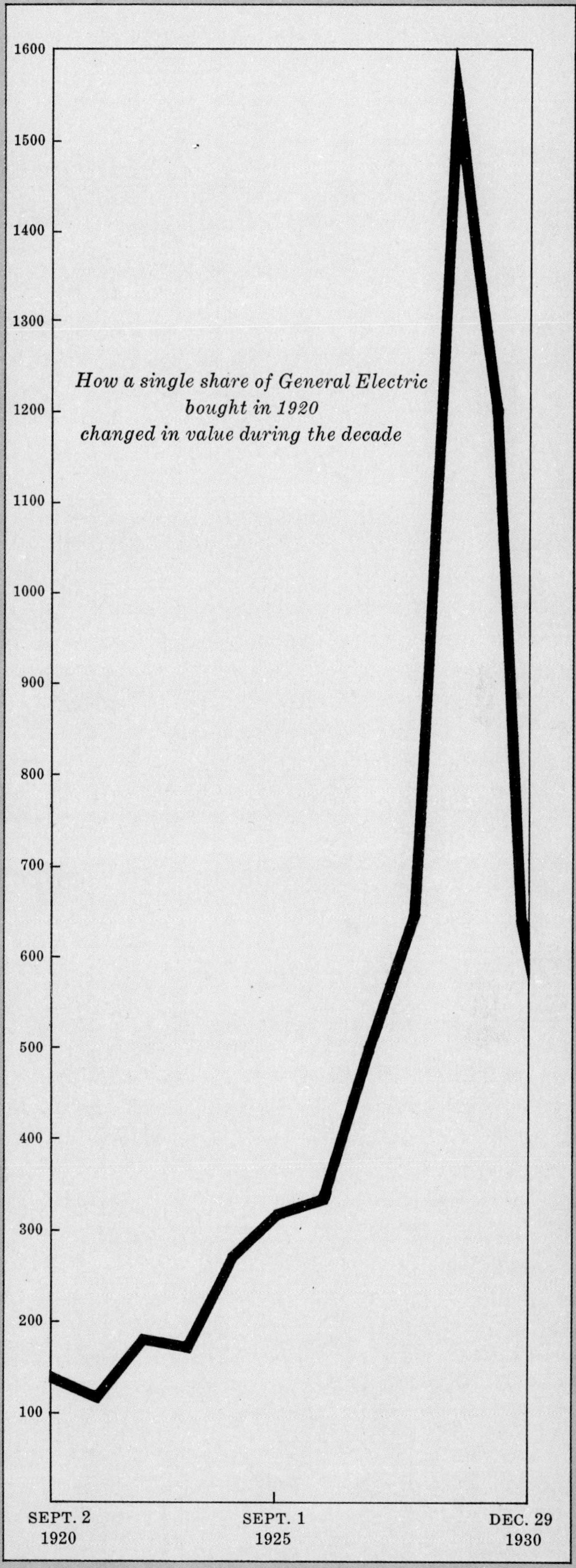

1600
1500
1400
1300
1200
1100
1000
900
800
700
600
500
400
300
200
100
How a single share of General Electric bought in 1920 changed in value during the decade
SEPT. 2 1920
SEPT. 1 1925
DEC. 29 1930

Black Tuesday, October 29, 1929, cost the stock list (left) $14 billion; the crash sent General Electric, a typical loser, plummeting (chart).

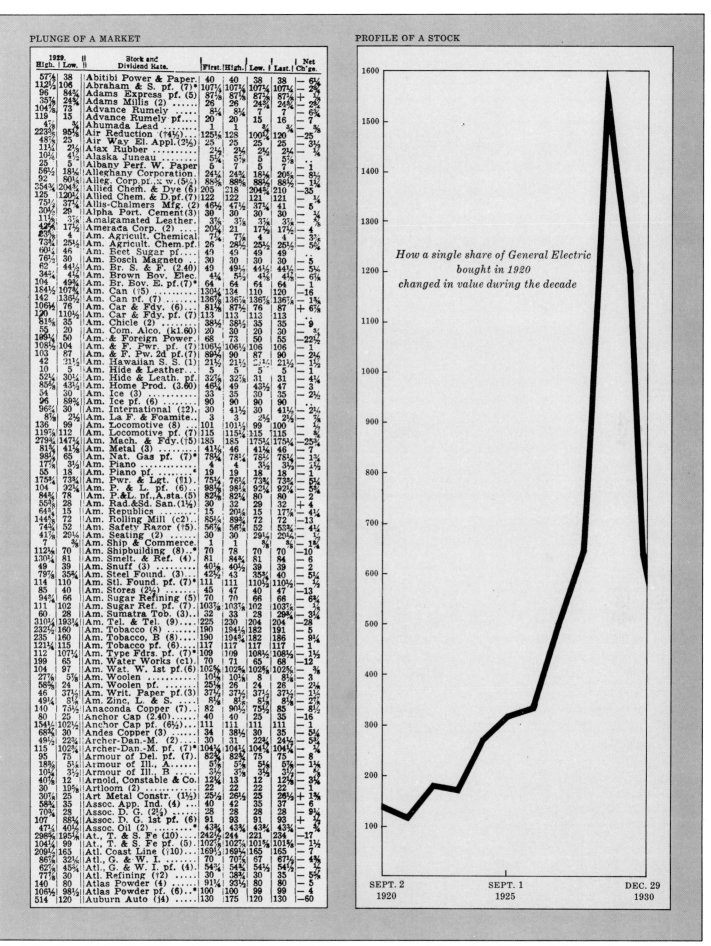

WORST STOCK CRASH STEMMED BY BANKS; 12,894,650-SHARE DAY SWAMPS MARKET; LEADERS CONFER, FIND CONDITIONS SOUND

FINANCIERS EASE TENSION

Five Wall Street Bankers Hold Two Meetings at Morgan Office.

Wall Street Optimistic After Stormy Day; Clerical Work May Force Holiday Tomorrow

Confidence in the soundness of the stock market structure, notwithstanding the upheaval of the last few days, was voiced last night by bankers and other financial leaders. Sentiment as expressed by the heads of some of the largest banking institutions and by industrial executives as well was distinctly cheerful and the feeling was general that the worst had been seen. Wall Street ended the day in an optimistic frame of mind.

The opinion of brokers was unanimous that the selling had got ... inherent weakness in the market

LOSSES RECOVERED IN PART

Upward Trend Starts With 200,000-Share Order for Steel.

TICKERS LAG FOUR HOU...

STOCKS GAIN AS MARKET IS ... BANKERS PLEDGE CONTINUE... HOOVER SAYS BUSINESS BA...

President Hoover Issues a Statement of Reassurance On Continued Prosperity of Fundamental Business

Special to The New York Times.

WASHINGTON, Oct. 25.—A reassuring statement that the fundamental business of the country was on a sound and prosperous basis was made by President Hoover at the White House this afternoon. It was made in reply to questions by newspaper men asking his opinion on the possible effect on the nation's prosperity of yesterday's collapse in the stock market.

Prior to his announcement, the President ... received detailed reports of th... the current ...

TR... 5,9...

Weird Roar Surges From Exchange Floor During Trading in a Reco...

BROKERS IN UPROAR AS MARKET BOILS

1,000 Mill Madly on Floor of Exchange and Thunder of Voices Is Heard Outside.

FURIOUS PACE BEFORE GONG

Then Perspiring Traders With Torn Collars Stand Limply or Jump and Laugh.

CROWDS SURGE IN ST...

Time to Buy Stocks, Says Raskob; Sees Only Temporary Effect on Business

John J. Raskob, one of the country's leading industrial and political leaders, declared last night in a statement to THE NEW YORK TIMES that many stocks are selling at bargain prices and that he and his friends are buyers of stocks. It may be stated in this conection that Mr. ... stock ... lid not ... that ... which ... afety. ... desk ... great ... con... ...uring

list is filled with stocks selling at real bargain prices.

"In a panic, whether in a theatre fire or the stock market, people lose their heads and go too far, which always results in needless and unnecessary suffering.

"Prudent investors are now buying stocks in huge quantities and will profit handsomely when this hysteria is over and our people have opportunity in calmer moments to appreciate the great stability of business by reason of the sound fundamental economic conditions existing in this great country.

"The pendulum has swung too far. The list is filled with bargains and ... friends and I are all buying ...

...asked if he be... ...stock

SENATORS STIRRED BY MARKET BREAK

King Presses His Proposal for Investigation of Federal Reserve System.

GLASS SEES VIEWS BACKED

Plans to Offer Measure for Tax on Sales as Tariff Bill Rider—Action Unlikely Till Decem...

Special to The New York Ti...

WASHINGTON, Oct. 24.—T... ...r collapse of the stock ... ...ay caused a revival in the ... suggestions for legislative ... curb credit for speculation ... ...endment of the National B... Federal Reserve acts to ... ...lits used in the stock m... ...ong with such proposals ... Senators advocated a th... ...stigation of the Federal ... ...system, as proposed

in stirring up interest in his pending resolution offered last May for an investigation of the Federal Reserve System. He said he would insist upon action by the Senate Banking and Currency Committee in the December session.

Immediate Inquiry Unlikely.

Senator Norbeck of South Dakota, chairman of that committee, declared that the committee apparently would favor an inquiry in the regular session, but there was little probability that it would be recommended in the present session. At this time the Senate is absorbed in the tariff bill.

Senator King said:

"Gambling in stock has become a national disease. This malady reaches all classes of people, from preachers to stable boys. Only a short time ago in all circles every one was talk...

raised the r... that business... sult that n... secured by ... tions for s... ment.

"In my ... meets in De... searching in... nancial syst... tion of cre... Federal Res... which inve... ating, the c... Stock Exch... matters wh... fare and p... Senator G... "The pres... ly to Charl... That man ... is responsi... tion. Had ... acted and ...

Crowds See M...

CROWDS AT TICKERS SEE FORTUNES WANE

Other Investors Sit Silently in ... Movies

Women T... Say Th...

The women ... took up the pas... seemed yesterd... returning to br... uptown offices ... firms, irritable ... 3 o'clock the g... remarks was th... forever.

Stock broker... women specul... losers. Many c... most worried ... They pushed ... crowded rooms ... quotations an... brokers for th... In one office ... chins asked a ... a quotation, ... marked: "You ... gentleman." S... Another wor... into the same ... loudly that sh... seemed proud ... and went arou...

...upraised as bi... It looked like ... A state of ... sweeps over g... games, at pri... valuted room ... self electrica...

STOCK PRICES SLUMP $14,000,000,000 IN NATION-WIDE STAMPEDE TO UNLOAD; BANKERS TO SUPPORT MARKET TOD...

Sixteen Leading Issues Down $2,893,520,108; Tel. & Tel. and Steel Among Heaviest Losers

A shrinkage of $2,893,520,108 in the open market value of the shares of sixteen representative companies resulted from yesterday's sweeping decline on the New York Stock Exchange.

American Telephone and Telegraph was the heaviest loser, $448,905,162 having been lopped off of its total value. United States Steel common, traditional bellwether of the stock market, made its greatest nose-dive in recent years by falling from a high of 202½ to a low of 185. In a feeble last-minute rally it snapped back to 186, at which it closed, showing a net loss of 17½ points. This represented for the 8,131,055 shares of common stock outstanding a total loss in value of $142,293,446.

In the following table are shown the day's net depreciation in the outstanding shares of the sixteen companies referred to:

Issues.	Shares Listed.	Losses in Points.	Depreciation.
American Radiator	10,096,289	10⅝	$104,748,997
American Tel. & Tel.	13,203,093	34	448,905,162
Commonwealth & Southern	30,764,468	3⅛	96,138,962
Columbia Gas & Electric	8,477,307	22	186,500,754
Consolidated Gas	11,451,188	20	229,023,760
DuPont E. I.	10,322,481	16⅝	109,030,625
Eastman Kodak	2,229,703	41⅞	93,368,813
General Electric	7,211,484	47½	342,545,49
General Motors	43,500,000	6¾	293,625,00
International Nickel	13,777,408	7⅞	108,497,08
New York Central	4,637,086	22⅝	104,914,07
Standard Oil of New Jersey	24,843,643	8	198,749,1
Union Carbide & Carbon	8,730,173	20	174,615,4
United States Steel	8,131,055	17½	142,293,4
United Gas Improvement	18,646,835	6	111,881,
...inghouse Elec. & Mfg.	2,589,265	34½	88,682,
			$2,893,520

... table are typical, but ... Some of ...

PREMIER ISSUES HA...

Unexpected Tor... Liquidation Rocks Mark...

DAY'S SALES

STOCKS MOUNT IN STRONG ALL-DAY RALLY; ROCKEFELLER BUYING HEARTENS MARKET; 2-DAY CLOSING ORDERED TO EASE STRAIN

Stocks Recover Nearly Half of Two Days' Losses; Total Gain in 16 Leading Issues Is $2,367,986,611

A group of sixteen representative stocks, which lost $2,893,520,108 in open market value in Monday's slump on the New York Stock Exchange and which showed almost as great a depreciation in Tuesday's break, recovered $2,367,986,611 in value yesterday, or nearly half of the aggregate loss of the group for the two-day break.

GAINS UP TO 36 POINTS

Prices Climb Steadily as 10,727,320 Shares Are Traded in Day...

Weary Throngs in Brokers' Offices Ch...

EXHAUSTED CROWDS CHEER STOCK RISE

Joy Supplants Fear in 1,000 Brokers' Rooms as Tickers Record Turning of Tide.

EXCHANGE HOLIDAY HAILED

Tired Customers Look Forward to Sleep Long Deferred, Clerks to ...

Weary Runners Nap on Bank's Marble Floor; Mitchell Orders Chairs Brought for Them

The results of the terrific strain of a succession of record-breaking days culminating in Tuesday's enormous turnover of 16,410,030 shares have extended to all sections of Wall Street's personnel. Nowhere was this more strikingly illustrated than in the scenes which took place on the main banking floor of the National City Bank at 55 Wall Street.

Hundreds of weary messengers, their hands and pockets crammed with bundles of securities worth hundreds of thousands of dollars, crowd...

the bank, it would have been comparatively simple for some one to steal a wallet full of negotiable stocks from some sleeping messenger.

Mr. Mitchell quickly ordered the guards to rouse the messengers and had camp chairs brought in for them to sit upon. For the rest of the afternoon the main floor of the bank resembled a drowsy prayer meeting with the runners playing a species of "marching to Jerusalem" as they gradually edged closer and closer to the loan windows.

In other banks similar scenes were enacted on a somewhat smaller scale. The unprecedented volume of trading ...

ROBINSON BLAMES THE REPUBLICANS

Charges Hoover, Mellon and Coolidge Fostered Era of Disastrous Speculation.

SAYS NONE ACTED ON BREAK

"High Priests of Prosperity" at Fault in Their Optimistic State-...

A montage of conflicting news stories, alternately frightening and reassuring, suggests the wild confusion that accompanied the stock market crash.

The Golden Dawn of Total Advertising

Lionized and romanticized, the advertising men of the '20s were prone to forget how far their vocation had come since the turn of the century. In that dim recent past, advertising's function remained primarily and politely informative—to announce and describe a product interestingly, lest potential customers fail to buy out of abysmal ignorance. Most advertising was so restrained that one job-hunting copywriter got himself hired by uttering what then seemed to be a startlingly new and aggressive definition: "Advertising Is Salesmanship in Print!"

In that go-getter spirit, the soft sell hardened as competition increased apace with the volume and variety of manufactured goods. Concurrently, the mass-marketing revolution broke down the lingering vestiges of regional merchandising, making it possible to advertise national brands in national magazines—this with the newly added impact of full-color printing. Thus the great postwar boom ushered in the age of all-out advertising. By 1925 the magazines and newspapers owed 70 per cent of their total income of $1.3 billion to ad revenue.

Under the tempering heat of competition, the modern advertising agency emerged in the '20s as a sophisticated team of high-paid specialists. Ad agencies earned their commissions by doing far more than creating and placing ads; their various experts often named, packaged, priced and promoted the distribution of the product. Great ad men could, and did, bestow instant success on fledgling products and sick businesses. Albert Lasker, the brilliant owner of the Lord & Thomas agency, was largely responsible in 1920 for selling America a rather shopworn firm and its untested new product—the Republican party and Warren G. Harding. And the rewards for success were fabulous. Lord & Thomas' resident genius, Claude C. Hopkins, who was widely regarded as the first and greatest of the great copywriters, took home as much as $300,000 in annual salary and commissions.

Marking the ads of the '20s were several traits that they shared with the decade itself, such as brashness and a lack of scruples. Many ads trafficked in quasi-factual, pseudo-scientific details: a mouthwash boasted the approval of exactly 45,512 doctors, none of them named, and a shaving cream stated with weighty significance that it expanded 250 times upon contact with water. Another phenomenon was the popularity of testimonial ads, which brought fees of up to $5,000 to celebrities in every field. Composer George Gershwin, actress Constance Talmadge and a heroic steamship captain all declared, in suspiciously similar language, that Lucky Strike was their cigarette because it protected the throat from coughing and the waistline from an unhealthy appetite for fattening sweets.

But the decade's dominant and identifying trend in advertising was the increasing use of psychology, the deepening appeal to the secret emotions that motivated people to buy. If any single ad epitomized the trend and solemnized its acceptance, it was Ned Jordan's 173-word classic, "Somewhere West of Laramie" (opposite).

Jordan was a copywriter-turned-manufacturer: trained in the "nuts-and-bolts" school of auto advertising, he had given in to an urge to produce cars himself. One day he caught a glimpse of a custom-built roadster that showman Flo Ziegfeld had ordered for actress Billie Burke, and on the strength of rough sketches he raised $400,000, capital enough to buy parts and assemble some rakish, aluminum-bodied cars. Then Jordan launched his ad.

"Somewhere West of Laramie" broke all the rules. It offered no data on the Jordan's brakes or carburetor; it made no grandiose claims of power or elegance. But the ad firmly planted in the readers' minds a connection between the Jordan and a pleasant feeling of freedom, excitement, romantic adventure. That was enough. Jordan's cars were too costly to sell in volume, but, as Jordan later said, "We *did* make a lot of money *awfully* fast."

As the decade wore on, psychological insights—particularly the realization that fear was a wonderful persuader —were applied with increasing effectiveness, as shown by the ads on following pages. The practice was not, to be sure, admired by everyone. But even the malcontents agreed with a cheerful squib in the Kansas City *Journal-Post:* "Advertising and mass production are the twin cylinders that keep the motor of modern business in motion."

Somewhere West of Laramie

SOMEWHERE west of Laramie there's a broncho-busting, steer-roping girl who knows what I'm talking about.

She can tell what a sassy pony, that's a cross between greased lightning and the place where it hits, can do with eleven hundred pounds of steel and action when he's going high, wide and handsome.

The truth is—the Playboy was built for her.

Built for the lass whose face is brown with the sun when the day is done of revel and romp and race.

She loves the cross of the wild and the tame.

There's a savor of links about that car—of laughter and lilt and light—a hint of old loves—and saddle and quirt. It's a brawny thing—yet a graceful thing for the sweep o' the Avenue.

Step into the Playboy when the hour grows dull with things gone dead and stale.

Then start for the land of real living with the spirit of the lass who rides, lean and rangy, into the red horizon of a Wyoming twilight.

JORDAN

JORDAN MOTOR CAR COMPANY, *Inc., Cleveland, Ohio*

Jordan's famous ad used vague, poetic prose to glamorize its cars. Dubbed "word-magic," the new style became a standard tool for selling costly items.

Naturally Lovable

"That Schoolgirl Complexion"

—is kept and safeguarded by thousands through following this simple rule in daily skin care

MODERN beauty culture, today, starts largely with choosing a bland complexion soap.

That's the reason millions use Palmolive—a soap made solely to safeguard the skin.

In America, it is the largest selling toilet soap. In France, it is one of the two largest—the "imported" soap in beauty-wise Paris, that is supplanting French soaps by the score!

As more women become skilled in the ways of beauty, more and more turn to natural ways in skin care.

That means a clean skin; pores kept free of accumulations to perform their functions *naturally*.

Thus modern beauty culture starts with soap and water; its only secret being the KIND of SOAP one uses—and how.

Palmolive is a beauty soap. A soap made of bland and soothing cosmetic oils, solely for one purpose; to safeguard the complexion. A soap made to be used freely, lavishly on the skin.

Used in the following way, it is credited with more beautiful skins, probably, than any other beauty method. Its results you see on every side today.

The rule to follow if guarding a good complexion is your goal

Wash your face gently with soothing Palmolive

Soap, massaging the lather softly into the skin. Rinse thoroughly, first with warm water, then with cold. If your skin is inclined to be dry, apply a touch of good cold cream—that is all. Do this regularly, and particularly in the evening. Use powder and rouge if you wish. But never leave them on over night. They clog the pores, often enlarge them, Blackheads and disfigurements often follow. They must be washed away.

Avoid this mistake

Do not use ordinary soaps in the treatment given above. Do not think any green soap, or one represented as of olive and palm oils, is the same as Palmolive.

And it costs but 10c the cake! So little that millions let it do for their bodies what it does for their faces. Obtain a cake today. Then note the amazing difference one week makes. The Palmolive Company (Del. Corp.), Chicago, Ill.

Retail Price 10c

Palmolive Soap is untouched by human hands until you break the wrapper—it is never sold unwrapped

KEEP THAT SCHOOLGIRL COMPLEXION

"A Skin You Love to Touch," by Clarence Underwood

You too, can have "A skin you love to touch"

A complete miniature set of the Woodbury skin preparations

For 25 cents we will send you a complete miniature set of the Woodbury skin preparations, containing samples of Woodbury's Facial Soap, Woodbury's Facial Cream, Woodbury's Cold Cream and Facial Powder; together with the treatment booklet, "A Skin You Love to Touch." Send for this set today. Address The Andrew Jergens Co., 1001 Spring Grove Ave., Cincinnati, Ohio. If you live in Canada, address The Andrew Jergens Co., Limited, 1001 Sherbrooke St., Perth, Ontario.

PERHAPS you have always longed for a beautiful skin—but felt that your skin was something you could not change.

You are mistaken; *your skin is what you make it.*

Every day it is changing in spite of you; old skin dies and new takes its place. This new skin you can make what you will!

If some special condition of your skin is giving you trouble—find the treatment that will overcome this trouble in the booklet of famous treatments that is wrapped around every cake of Woodbury's Facial Soap. Begin using this treatment tonight. You will be surprised to see how quickly you can free your skin from faults that have always troubled you.

Get a cake of Woodbury's today. A 25-cent cake lasts a month or six weeks. The Andrew Jergens Co., Cincinnati, New York, and Perth, Ontario.

Woodbury's Facial Soap

Copyright, 1922, by The Andrew Jergens Co.

"Quick, Henry, the Flit!"

The human fly is a bit unbalanced for the moment, and small wonder! Henry has probably mislaid the familiar yellow can with the black band, and another good man is about to be sunk. It won't be the first time a mosquito has ruined a good day's work or a good night's sleep. Seriously (if you *can* be serious in Life) modern people aren't being bothered by flies, mosquitoes, and other insects this summer. They spray Flit, and let the insects do the worrying.

Clean-smelling Flit spray is stainless, and harmless to humans; but quick-death to all insects.

FLIT

The pause that refreshes

Drink **Coca-Cola**
Delicious and Refreshing

The Coca-Cola Company, Atlanta, Ga.

EACH busy day tends down hill from that top-of-the-morning feeling with which you begin. Don't whip yourself as the day begins to wear. Pause and refresh yourself with an ice-cold Coca-Cola, and be off to a fresh start. ▼ ▼ ▼ The wholesome refreshment of Coca-Cola has made it the one great drink of the millions. A perfect blend of many flavors, it has

IT HAD TO BE GOOD

OVER 8 MILLION A DAY

a flavor all its own—delicious to taste and, more than that, with a cool after-sense of refreshment. ▼ ▼ ▼ It is ready, cold and tingling, at fountains and refreshment stands around the corner from anywhere.

THE BEST SERVED DRINK IN THE WORLD
A pure drink of natural flavors served ice-cold in its own bottle—the distinctive Coca-Cola bottle. Every bottle is sterilized, filled and sealed air-tight by automatic machines, without the touch of human hands—insuring purity and wholesomeness.

TO GET WHERE IT IS

I'll tell the world
They Satisfy

Chesterfield
CIGARETTES

—and the blend can't be copied

Liggett & Myers Tobacco Co.

"I'D WALK A MILE FOR A CAMEL"

—but a "MISS" is as Good as a MILE

GOOD TO THE LAST DROP

ON THE GREAT WHITE FLEET

In the blue Caribbean

SOLD ONLY IN SEALED TIN CANS-CONVENIENT TO OPEN AND USE

On the majestic ships of the United Fruit Company's Great White Fleet—famous for the excellence of their cuisine—with "Every Passenger a Guest"—Maxwell House Coffee is always served.

Sail on any of these super ships, and at your first meal, as you enjoy that delicious, fragrant coffee to the very last drop, call your waiter and ask: "What coffee is this?" He will tell you: "Maxwell House."

Go where you will—on fast, famous trains, to better hotels and restaurants, on great steamships, to the finest of private homes and to the humble cottage by the side of the road—and you will find within your cup of Maxwell House Coffee the fruit of a half century of search for flavor.

The finest coffees of the world are roasted, blended and packed in our six great plants, and sealed in the famous blue tin.

Also Maxwell House Tea.

CHEEK-NEAL COFFEE CO.,
Nashville,   Houston,   Jacksonville,   Richmond,   New York.

MAXWELL HOUSE COFFEE

Slogans old and new became familiar through repetition. Like others, "Good to the last drop" long outlived its creator: Theodore Roosevelt.

An Era of Giants

I see them walk by in a dream—Dempsey and Cobb and Ruth,

Tunney and Sande and Jones—Johnson and Matty and Young—

Alex and Tilden and Thorpe—was there a flash of youth

That gave us a list like this, when our first tributes were sung?

GRANTLAND RICE

This was the heroic era of American sports. Attendance at athletic events broke all records, and the champions of sport were known and loved throughout the land. "If St. Paul were living today," a prominent Methodist minister declared, "he would know Babe Ruth's batting average and what yardage Red Grange made."

And that applied to many others besides Ruth and Grange. Jack Dempsey, the grim Manassa Mauler, came out of the West to give boxing its first million-dollar gates. Bobby Jones and Bill Tilden took golf and tennis away from the country-club crowd and made them "important" sports. Swimmer Gertrude Ederle, Helen Wills, a tennis player, and golfer Glenna Collett showed that a woman's place was also in the sports pages.

One reason for the heightened interest in sport was the sudden emergence of the sports writer as a major figure on the literary scene—men such as Grantland Rice, Damon Runyon, Ring Lardner, Paul Gallico, John Kieran and Westbrook Pegler. These experts were occasionally assisted by outsiders like H. L. Mencken and even George Bernard Shaw. (Shaw described the game of baseball as a combination of the "best features of that primitive form of cricket known as Tip and Run with those of

lawn tennis, Puss-in-the-Corner, and Handel's *Messiah*.")

The great writers recorded the deeds of the great athletes. One early beneficiary was that giant of giants, Babe Ruth. "After the Black Sox scandal," wrote W. O. McGeehan, "Babe Ruth with his bat pounded baseball back into popularity. He swings with the utmost sincerity. When he hits the ball it goes into wide-open spaces. When he misses, he misses with vehement sincerity."

By 1927, when he hit his high-water mark of 60 home runs, Babe Ruth was a better-known American to most foreigners than Calvin Coolidge, and he rivaled the dashing Prince of Wales as the most photographed man in the world. Kieran was moved to this bit of hero-worshipping doggerel, typical of the sports-page exaggeration of the era: "My voice may be loud above the crowd / And my words just a bit uncouth, / But I'll stand and shout till the last man's out: / 'There never was a guy like Ruth!' "

The fact that the Babe was himself a bit uncouth—a wencher, imbiber, and notorious violator of training rules —bothered neither the writers nor the fans. He was simply the greatest ballplayer who ever lived, and he symbolized as no other man ever did the love affair that existed between the American public and the athletes of the 1920s.

Paul Gallico wrote of Ruth: "There has always been a magic about that gross, ugly, coarse, Gargantuan figure of a man and everything he did."

Red Grange, shown as a pro player, said, "The same fellows who advised me not to play professional wouldn't lend me a dollar if I were broke."

The Rock and the Redhead

Until the '20s, a fair number of Eastern sports writers believed that the only brand of college football worth writing about was played on the gridirons of Harvard, Yale and Princeton. And then along came Knute Rockne and Red Grange out of the Midwest to change their minds.

Rockne's superbly coached Notre Dame teams won 105 games and lost only 12 between 1919 and 1931. His locker-room exhortations became football lore; but his real renown rested on his ability to find—and make—fine football players. Four of the best were on his 1924 team; after that year's victory over Army, while groping for words to describe the small, swift Notre Dame backfield, Grantland Rice typed: "Outlined against a blue-gray October sky, the Four Horsemen rode again. In dramatic lore they are known as Famine, Pestilence, Destruction and Death. These are only aliases. Their real names are Stuhldreher, Miller, Crowley and Layden."

But even the best players Rockne could produce were overshadowed by Red Grange, the "Galloping Ghost" of Illinois. A three-time All-American, Grange helped dedicate Illinois' new stadium in 1924 by personally demolishing a fine Michigan team with touchdown runs of 95, 67, 55 and 45 yards the first four times he carried the ball. Within hours after he stripped off his famous No. 77 jersey for the last time in 1925, Grange signed a contract to play professionally. "I do not like football well enough to play it for nothing," he explained. Playing it for about $1,000 a minute, Grange was a millionaire in just three years.

---

*A*fter his team had taken a first-half shellacking and sat waiting for the blast, Rockne merely poked his head in the door of the dressing room and remarked quietly, "Oh, excuse me, ladies! I thought this was the Notre Dame team." PAUL GALLICO

What a football player—this man Red Grange. He is melody and symphony. He is crashing sound. He is brute force.

DAMON RUNYON

KNUTE ROCKNE

31

Man O'War's giant stride ate up 27 feet at every leap, and the jockey's toughest job often was to pace the big horse when he tried to run all out.

"De Mostest Hoss"

The sports writers dubbed him "Big Red," but his groom, Will Harbut, called him "de mostest hoss" and that was a better description of Man O'War. He was an amazing combination of size (1,150 pounds) and speed (five American records in 1920 alone), with an appetite so great that he reportedly was fed with a bit in his mouth to slow down his eating. Man O'War won 20 of his 21 starts in 1919 and 1920; at least once he ran away from the field by 100 lengths, a figure in keeping with the odds in his favor, which three times reached 1 to 100. In the one race he lost—to a horse named, naturally, Upset—he was victimized by a poor start and was gaining rapidly at the finish. Earl Sande, the premier jockey of the decade, rode Man O'War only once and never forgot it. "That day, I knew I was riding the greatest horse ever bred for running," he said. The *New York Tribune* ran the following account of Man O'War's most exciting victory in 1920.

Man O'War proved himself the horse of eternity at Aqueduct yesterday afternoon. Lucky indeed was he who can say he saw Man O'War on July 10, 1920. He saw the greatest race of turf history won by the greatest horse. But for this super-horse, John P. Grier might today be heralded as the equine champion of the age. He ran a race that would have beaten any horse that ever looked through a bridle—except Man O'War. From start to finish, every post of the journey was passed in record time. And until almost the very end it seemed that Grier might win. For the first time in his racing career the sleek chestnut sides of Man O'War felt the cut of the whip. Kummer applied the lash with right good will. And Man O'War, roused to the idea that something vital was at stake, responded as the great horse that he is. He charged at his rival with all the power of his marvellous frame and simply broke the heart of as game a three-year-old as this country will see in many a day. W. J. MACBETH

The Noble Experiment

No person shall, on or after the date when the 18th Amendment to the Constitution of the United States goes into effect, manufacture, sell, barter, transport, import, export, deliver, furnish or possess any intoxicating liquor except as authorized in this act.

TITLE II, SECTION 3, NATIONAL PROHIBITION ACT

The 1920s were scarcely two weeks old when the United States launched on one of the maddest follies of a mad decade. On January 16, the 18th Amendment became the law of the land, making liquor, beer and wine illegal throughout the country. With it came the National Prohibition Act (popularly called the Volstead Act, for its author), by which the Amendment was to be enforced.

President Hoover called the Amendment "a great social and economic experiment, noble in motive." Noble though it may have been, seldom has law been more flagrantly violated. Not only did Americans continue to manufacture, barter and possess alcohol; they drank more of it. Women, to whom the saloon had been off limits, trooped into Prohibition's invention, the speak-easy, where they consumed quantities of Prohibition's new potion, the cocktail. Moonshining, formerly carried on in the hills by country folk for their own convenience, became big business. So did smuggling; hundreds of ships were anchored three miles off the Atlantic Coast in a line from Maine to Florida, dispensing liquor to anyone who chose to come out by rowboat, skiff or speedboat.

Officers of the law conspired with the drinkers to make a travesty of Prohibition. Some of the agents were honest, hardworking men trying to do a thankless job. But Congressman Fiorello H. La Guardia, declaring that it would take a police force of 250,000 to enforce Prohibition in New York City, added sourly that another 200,000 would be required to police the police. In Philadelphia, grafters were said to have pocketed $20 million in three years; in Detroit they hauled in two million dollars a year. In Chicago gangsters held the city in thrall. In San Francisco, a jury trying a Prohibition case was found drinking up the liquor that had been used in court as evidence. In Texas, just a few months after the start of Prohibition, a still turning out 130 gallons of whiskey a day was found operating on the farm of Senator Morris Sheppard, author of the 18th Amendment. In Washington the Prohibition Bureau had the highest turnover of officers of any government agency—some 10,000 men held 3,000 jobs in six years—a fact that elicited from one who remained the rueful comment that the Bureau was running "a training school for bootleggers."

"If you think this country ain't dry," remarked the comedian Will Rogers, "just watch 'em vote; if you think this country ain't wet, just watch 'em drink. You see, when they vote, it's counted, but when they drink, it ain't."

A padlock, grim symbol of Prohibition, hangs on the door of a saloon. Lest anyone miss the point, an agent hammers on a sign bearing the sad news.

Do It Yourself Booze

The temperance advocates, who cheered the death of the saloon only to see it replaced by the speak-easy, were in for yet another surprise: certain Americans who had always shied away from the rowdy barroom began to do something they had scarcely done before—drink at home. Half the fun was in making the booze themselves. For six or seven dollars, a portable still could be purchased in almost any hardware store. If the buyer didn't know how to use it, all he had to do was go to the public library, where he could find, on the open shelves, thousands of books, magazines, even government pamphlets, that described in detail the art of distillation. He could then go home and apply his new knowledge in his own kitchen, using for raw materials prunes, apples, bananas, watermelon, potato peelings, oats or barley.

But there were easier ways. It was a simple matter to get alcohol or ingredients that when mixed together would turn to alcohol, and the manufacturers of scores of products were only too happy to oblige. The vintners of California prospered all during Prohibition. Under the tutelage of a former Assistant Attorney General, who steered them through the ins and outs of the Prohibition law, they got out a legal product called Vine-Glo—a grape juice which, when put in the cellar and nursed for 60 days, turned into wine that was 15 per cent alcohol. Wine-growers even expanded their acreage during Prohibition, from

A Brick of Wine

This invention of a New York state vintner, a solid block of grape concentrate about the size of a pound of butter, made a more or less palatable drink when water was added. With it came a circular that solicitously warned the customer what he ought not to do— or else he would have wine, and that would be illegal.

Help for the Patient

Under the Volstead Act, alcohol for medicinal purposes was legal. Doctors prescribed it and druggists dispensed it freely; very soon it was being sold at the rate of a million gallons a year, and the number of "patients" soared. This was one scheme the Prohibition authorities hardly even tried to stop.

97,000 in 1919 to 681,000 in 1926, and in 1929 they got a loan from Uncle Sam to expand still more.

Beer was more of a problem, but the brewers, too, found a way. The Volstead Act allowed the manufacture of a concoction containing half of 1 per cent alcohol, called "near beer" (it had been named, according to a current gag, by a poor judge of distance). Nobody wanted near beer—it was tasteless and had no kick. But before long some smart brewer came up with the idea of halting the process of beer-making before there was any alcohol at all, and selling the half-brewed result, called wort, along with a package of yeast that would convey it the rest of the way. What with one thing and another, there was soon so much spirituous beverage being manufactured in the nation's basements, bathrooms and (for all anyone knew to the contrary) bedrooms that an anonymous poet was inspired to write in the New York *World:*

> *Mother makes brandy from cherries;*
> *Pop distills whiskey and gin;*
> *Sister sells wine from the grapes on our vine—*
> *Good grief, how the money rolls in!*

Pictured below are some of the other devices Americans turned to in an effort to quench their thirst during Prohibition. With the exception of that illegal can of alcohol *(third from left)* all observed the letter of the law.

Mix and Serve

"The contents of this package," said the label on the can of moonshine alcohol above, "is guaranteed to be distilled from grain only, is free from adulteration." Maybe it was and maybe not; many such products contained wood alcohol. Either way, the buyer added essence of juniper and got a gallon of gin.

Near Beer

Famous brewers, like Pabst (above), heeded the law by selling nothing but near beer. But hardly anyone drank it straight. Congressman Fiorello H. La Guardia, an ardent Wet, mixed his with alcoholic malt tonic from the drugstore, and triumphantly posed for his picture, pronouncing the result "delicious!"

Nunnally's
THE CANDY OF THE SOUTH

PERSONALITY
HAVANA FILLED

ORE

SMOKE Y-B CIGAR

DRINK Coca-Cola

A Dallas newsstand offers a variety of journals.

New Vigor in the Public Print

He was the editor of a tabloid "newspaper" but he loved his children. So he told them he was a burglar.

COLLEGE HUMOR, 1927

Their appetites for news whetted by a world war, their leisure augmented by the eight-hour day, their literacy rate climbing, Americans turned hungrily to the printed word. The newspapers gave them a rich and varied diet. From *The New York Times* they got top-notch foreign correspondence. In the New York *World* they could read Franklin P. Adams, Heywood Broun and other superlatively witty columnists. The exposé of evil-doing in high places became the mark of many a good paper: the *St. Louis Post-Dispatch* forced an allegedly corrupt federal judge to resign; the *Indianapolis Times* exposed Indiana's Ku Klux Klan leader as a murderer. Newspaper circulation boomed; the total for the nation was about 25 million when the decade started and about 40 million at its close. The first of the tabloids arrived in 1919, with the most lurid news coverage the country had ever known; their competition shook the old business to its roots.

Magazines, meanwhile, experienced an unprecedented boom. While *The Saturday Evening Post, Collier's*, the *National Geographic*, the *Literary Digest* and other old mass-market giants reached circulation peaks, new magazines began shaking the established order by their candor and iconoclasm. The *American Mercury*, founded in 1924 and edited by curmudgeons Henry L. Mencken *(page 210)* and George Jean Nathan, lambasted Rotarians, Babbitts, Fundamentalists and the rest of what Mencken called the "booboisie." *Time*, the first of the news magazines, started in 1923. The *New Yorker*, launched in 1925, tackled American life with a deft, wicked, penetrating wit. Several old-timers were at the forefront of this vigorous journalism: the *Forum* sought out debates on troubling issues and staid old *Scribner's* was banned in Boston for running Ernest Hemingway's *A Farewell to Arms* as a serial.

All was not highbrow, however; by 1926, Bernarr Macfadden's *True Story Magazine* (founded in 1919) was titillating a readership of nearly two million with tales of love among the shopgirls; a host of competing confession magazines sprang up in its wake.

The magazines poked fun at everything—including other magazines. To the *New Yorker's* condescending proclamation that it was not being published "for the old lady in Dubuque," *Time* commented loftily: "There is no provincialism so blatant as that of the metropolitan who lacks urbanity." In 1929 a series of cartoons in the humorous weekly *Life*, some of which are reproduced here, satirized, with sharp perception, a score of *Life's* competitors.

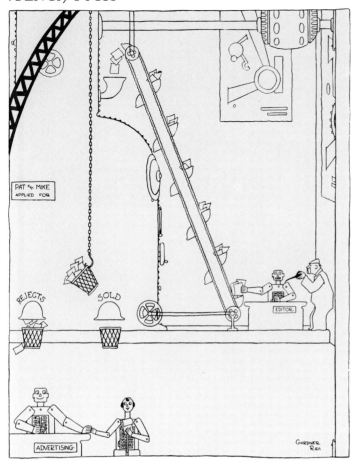

POPULAR MECHANICS

GOOD HOUSEKEEPING

COLLEGE HUMOR

TRUE CONFESSIONS

ATLANTIC MONTHLY

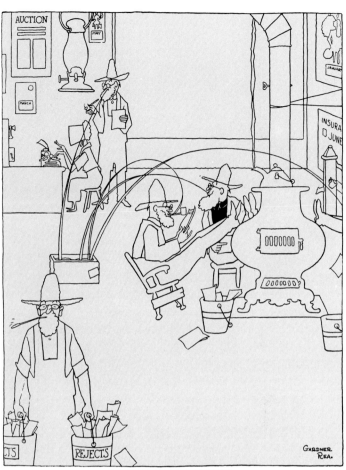

THE COUNTRY GENTLEMAN

THE NATIONAL GEOGRAPHIC

THE NEW YORKER

Names in the News

It was an era when anyone whose name was in the newspapers was automatically a celebrity. Whether he wanted the publicity or not, whether he was a scientist, cellist, senator or murderer—it didn't make any difference. The press and the radio were talking about him, and in the eyes of the public he had been touched with magic.

People felt they were on a first-name basis with Edward, Prince of Wales, and Queen Marie of Romania (both of whom paid splashy visits to the United States), and everyone everywhere discussed Albert Einstein's absentmindedness as though he were a neighbor. The man on the street referred casually to the way the great financier Bernard Baruch was playing the stock market or what Paris gowns the Vanderbilt ladies were buying. Evangelists like Billy Sunday and Aimee Semple McPherson, pilots like Eddie Rickenbacker, society playgirls like Peggy Hopkins Joyce, even Freud and advice-to-the-lovelorn columnist Dorothy Dix—all were known quantities, recognizable personalities, friendly faces.

One way for a public figure to make it big was to be—or appear to be—particularly average. Hiram Wesley Evans, the Imperial Wizard of the Ku Klux Klan, declared proudly that he was "the most average man in America," but there were many other men fiercely competing for that distinction. One contender in mid-decade was the President, Calvin Coolidge. In an age that was loud, extravagant and zany, the President was silent, frugal and drab. The son of a Vermont farmer, he seldom spoke in public (though his intimates said he was a maddening chatterbox in private) and he wore an expression that one quipster said had been "weaned on a pickle."

In order to underline just how average he was, Coolidge posed for news photographs showing him pitching hay on his farm (dressed, if one looked closely, in a suit and patent leather shoes). Perhaps Coolidge's appeal was best summarized by the political writer Walter Lippmann who observed that Americans "feel, I think, that they are stern, ascetic and devoted to plain living because they vote for a man who is. Thus we have attained a Puritanism de luxe in which it is possible to praise the classic virtues, while continuing to enjoy all the modern conveniences."

A different sort of popular hero was Jimmy Walker, the mayor of New York City. He was also conspicuously "average" but in a racy, big city way. He wrote lyrics for Tin Pan Alley, never started work before noon, kept show girls on the side, though he was married, and took seven vacations during his first two years in office. But *Outlook* magazine said of him, "Jimmy translated the problems of municipal government, a series of headaches to the average citizen, into simple musical comedy terms."

The prestige of the "average" man, however, took a serious beating in 1925 during the famous "Monkey Trial" in Dayton, Tennessee. The state of Tennessee had passed a law against teaching the theory of evolution in the public schools. (The theory was commonly—and wrongly—expressed by its detractors as holding that "man was descended from a monkey.") When a local teacher, John T. Scopes, was accused of breaking the law, Clarence Darrow, a famous lawyer, an agnostic and a champion of civil liberties, volunteered to defend him. The state was represented by William Jennings Bryan, a Fundamentalist who had been defeated three times as the Democratic candidate for the Presidency. Bryan liked to think he stood for the average man and relished his sobriquet, "The Great Commoner." The high point of the trial came when Darrow cross-examined Bryan about his religious beliefs. Bryan affirmed his literal interpretation of the Bible—that the world was created in 4004 B.C., that Jonah was swallowed by a big fish, that Eve was made out of Adam's rib. Bryan claimed that the purpose of the examination was "to cast ridicule on everybody who believes in the Bible," to which Darrow replied in a withering attack: "We have the purpose of preventing bigots and ignoramuses from controlling the education of the United States."

The Court convicted Scopes and the Tennesseeans applauded Bryan, but much of the world shook with laughter over the spectacle Bryan had made of himself. Bryan's notion that one honest, average man was worth a handful of experts had suffered a devastating blow, and soon after the trial "The Great Commoner" died, a shattered man.

Calvin Coolidge

A man with a flair for publicity, President Coolidge frequently made appearances rigged out in Indian feathers or cowboy clothes. Coolidge succeeded Warren G. Harding in office and sought to free his administration of the scandals that had plagued Harding. A Republican and a conservative, he once said that Government's "greatest duty and opportunity is not to embark on any new ventures."

Greta Garbo inspired such devotion that her fans were called "Garbomaniacs."

The Glamour of the Films

In an age of celebrities, the most glamorous of all were the movie stars. In the earliest days of the films, producers had tried to keep their actors anonymous lest they become popular and demand huge salaries. But by the '20s the movie makers had come to realize that a big name outdrew a good picture—and was worth big money. Soon a major attraction like Lillian Gish could ask for $400,000 a year.

By 1920 some 35 million Americans were going to the movies at least once a week, mainly to see melodramatic love stories and Westerns; in 1926 the first war films began to appear; and in 1927 gangster pictures started their vogue. The top movie personalities—whether they were cowboys, vamps, flappers, comedians, cops, robbers or swashbucklers—were now receiving about 32 million fan letters a year.

Every aspect of the stars' lives was followed with fascination. The marriage of Mary Pickford to Douglas Fairbanks in 1920 set off nationwide jubilation. When Charlie Chaplin visited England a year later, the British lined the docks to welcome him. Even animal stars were idolized; the dog Rin-Tin-Tin was voted most popular film performer in 1926. Perhaps the most fascinating of all the stars, however, was the publicity-shy Swedish actress Greta Garbo. She was so elusive and standoffish that studio press agents at first complained about how uncooperative she was being. Soon, however, it became clear that her very insistence on privacy was an enormous asset, and the legend of Garbo "The Sphinx" was launched.

Rudolph Valentino, most famous of the screen lovers, gives a sulky pout in his next-to-last role, as Dubrovski in "The Eagle."

The Hollywood Sex Queens

Alla Nazimova invested her life savings to produce "Salome."

Pola Negri, exotic and hot-tempered, dances in "Bella Donna."

Gloria Swanson flirts in "Her Gilded Cage," a 1922 tearjerker.

Ziegfeld Girl Mae Murray was a glittering "Merry Widow."

The Lovers

Dolores Costello and John Barrymore appeared together in "Sea Beast."

An intense Rudolph Valentino embraces Alla Nazimova.

Janet Gaynor and Charles Farrell starred in "Seventh Heaven," a 1927 film.

Greta Garbo and John Gilbert make love in "Flesh and the Devil," which established her as a star.

Vilma Banky and Ronald Colman act the title roles in "Two Lovers."

The younger set: Douglas Fairbanks Jr. and Joan Crawford.

Forlorn and cold, Charlie Chaplin huddles by his shack in "The Gold Rush."

Harold Lloyd, perched precariously on a clock above the street, flirts with danger in "Safety Last."

Buster Keaton, who never smiled on screen, bathes in a scene from "The Three Ages," in which he was cast as a prehistoric cave man.

Fame, Fortune and Folly

Clarence Tillman, 17, local high school student, put 40 sticks of chewing gum in his mouth at one time, sang "Home, Sweet Home," and between verses of the song, drank a gallon of milk.

UNITED PRESS DISPATCH FROM WARSAW, INDIANA

During the '20s Americans were torn by two contrary desires: the urge to be like everyone else, and the urge to be utterly different. For many people, both yearnings were neatly satisfied by the zany fads that swept the country during the decade. By taking up the latest craze, an American could demonstrate that he was a good conformist. On the other hand, by being a little more fad-happy than his neighbors—by becoming the local expert on mah-jongg rules or the best at doing crossword puzzles or the most indefatigable marathon dancer—he could prove that he really was unlike anyone else, unique in his chosen field.

In previous decades, the pace of pop culture had been more measured; fads and habits had changed, but only very gradually. During the '20s, however, the advent of nationwide radio networks and the growing use of syndicated columns helped to disseminate with whirlwind speed news of the most recent parlor game or endurance contest. Simultaneously, publicists perfected ways of focusing the full glare of the mass media on their pet projects.

Crossword puzzles were a prime example. Two young publishers, Richard L. Simon and M. Lincoln Schuster, brought out a collection of the puzzles as their first book. Skillful promoters, Simon and Schuster attached pencils to each volume, devised an ingenious advertising campaign—and watched their profits soar. Suddenly everyone was crazy about crosswords. The Baltimore and Ohio Railroad placed dictionaries on trains for the convenience of puzzlers. College teams competed in tournaments and in New York thousands of fans cheered two crossword finalists in a national contest. The University of Kentucky offered a course in crossword puzzles because, as the dean said, they were "educational, scientific, instructive and mentally stimulative, as well as entertaining." An ingenious minister in Utah cast his sermon into a crossword that was solved by the congregation during the service.

Crosswords were just one of scores of fads that swept the country. Contract bridge, Yo-yo's and roller-skating became popular manias. People competed in rocking-chair derbies, dance marathons and cross-country races. Others hoped to win fleeting fame by becoming the world's champion pea-eater or kisser or talker. A man in Minnesota claimed a world's record after he bobbed up and down in the water 1,843 times, prompting *The Saturday Evening Post* to comment wryly that Americans were "first in war, first in peace, first in tree sitting, gum chewing, peanut pushing and bobbing up and down in water."

Pursuing a great fad of the era, a girl looks up "Egyptian Sun God" in the world's smallest crossword-puzzle dictionary, strapped to her wrist.

"Shipwreck" Kelly sways above a theater in Union City, New Jersey.

Flagpole Sitting

"The Luckiest Fool Alive," as he called himself, was "Shipwreck" Kelly, the era's most famous flagpole sitter. A former boxer who fought under the name Sailor Kelly, he was knocked out so often that fans started shouting, "The sailor's been shipwrecked again"—thus, his name.

Shipwreck started sitting on flagpoles in 1924 in Hollywood (where else?), where a theater had hired him to draw crowds. Soon he was booked by scores of hotels desiring publicity. Balanced on a small disk equipped with stirrups to keep him from falling off, Kelly took five-minute catnaps every hour and subsisted on liquids hoisted up to him on ropes. In 1929 Kelly put in a total of 145 days on various flagpoles around the country.

All that was lacking in Shipwreck's career was romance—and that came to him one day in Dallas when a hotel elevator girl indignantly slapped a passenger who called Kelly a fool. Kelly, sitting on the hotel's flagpole, asked to meet the 18-year-old girl. She was hoisted up for a chat;

The grit and stamina evidenced by your endurance from July 20th to 30th, a period of 10 days, 10 hours, 10 minutes and 10 seconds atop of the 22 foot pole in the rear of your home shows that the old pioneer spirit of early America is being kept alive by the youth of today.   WILLIAM F. BROENING, MAYOR OF BALTIMORE

---

after he came down they were married. Six years later the girl sued for a divorce, charging that his career had come between them. "What's the use of having a husband," she asked the judge, "unless he comes home nights?"

Despite such minor setbacks, Shipwreck's fame continued to grow, and many imitators sprang up—particularly, for some reason, in Baltimore. The Baltimore flagpole madness began when 15-year-old Avon Foreman set up an 18-foot hickory sapling in his back yard and perched on top. Others followed suit, and during one week in 1929 Baltimore had no fewer than 20 pole-sitters (17 boys and 3 girls). The city's proud mayor visited many of the arboreal Baltimoreans and sent the letter excerpted above to young Avon Foreman, who had started it all.

Baltimore's pride, Avon Foreman sits on a platform that he mounted on a pole. During his feat, he received encouragement from some 5,000 neighbors.

Decked out in Oriental finery, a galaxy of film starlets gathers around a mah-jongg table at "the shrine of the Chinese God of Luck" in Los Angeles.

The Mah-Jongg Craze

In 1922 an ancient Chinese game called mah-jongg invaded America. By the following year millions of people, particularly members of ladies' clubs, were shouting "Pung!" and "Chow!" and other bizarre words at one another. Many enthusiasts refused to play without the proper Oriental accessories, and sales of Chinese robes soared.

A sort of combination of dice and dominoes, mah-jongg required a set of 144 tiles, originally manufactured only in China. In 1923 mah-jongg sets outsold radios; the demand was so great that the Chinese ran out of the shinbones of calves, which were used to make the tiles. The beef-packers of Chicago had to ship bones from their slaughterhouses to China so that artisans there could carve them into tiles and then send them back to the United States. American efficiency experts also helped the Chinese set up mah-jongg assembly lines. A good set manufactured in China might sell in the U.S. for as much as $500, although American-made copies fashioned in celluloid could be bought for only a few dollars.

The game's notorious complexities were satirized by Eddie Cantor, who sang in the revue *Kid Boots* a song titled "Since Ma Is Playing Mah Jong." One stanza went:

If you want to play the game I'll tell you what to do,
Buy a silk kimona and begin to raise a queue;
Get yourself a book of rules and study till it's clear,
And you'll know the game when you've got whiskers down to here.

As the song implies, the rules of play, also made in China, were inscrutable and subject to constant change. During the decade more than 20 rule books were issued, often wildly at variance with one another. On the West Coast, where the game was particularly popular, the Seattle *Daily Times* printed a mah-jongg column in which new rule interpretations were offered. One rule book complained that the game was being ruined by "expert" instructors who made up regulations as they went along. "Even the Chinese in America are not without reproach," the book said, "for certain of them have posed as professional teachers although their acquaintance with the game has been of shorter duration than that of many Americans."

A Dance to Exhaustion

"Of all the crazy competitions ever invented," the New York *World* remarked in 1923, "the dancing marathon wins by a considerable margin of lunacy." The object of these strange contests was to see which couple could outdance— or outlive—all the others. All across the country men and women staggered in near-exhaustion to the tune of fox trots played by Victrolas or seedy little bands.

The dancers sometimes competed for prizes of as much as several thousand dollars. The spectators came to see the antics of the performers. In order to keep their partners awake, dancers would kick and punch them and offer them smelling salts and ice packs. Unprincipled contestants would slip their rivals drinks containing sleeping pills or laxatives. After seven or eight days of painful plodding (in 1930 a Chicago marathon went on for 119 days) dancers would often start acting peculiarly. Girls would come to hate their partners so much they would scream

There is nothing inspiring in seeing an extremely tired pretty girl in a worn bathrobe, dingy white stockings in rolls about scuffing felt slippers, her eyes half shut, her arms hung over her partner's shoulders, drag aching feet that seemed glued to the floor in one short, agonizing step after another. NEW YORK *WORLD,* 1923

when they saw them. One man in New York suffered from delusions that someone was picking his pocket; he was disqualified when he ran off the floor and down the street chasing an imaginary culprit.

One of the few contestants who never seemed to suffer from mental problems or aching feet was Mary "Hercules" Promitis of Pittsburgh. She never divulged how she retained her sanity, but she did reveal how she kept her feet in shape. Learning that bare-fisted prize fighters often pickled their hands, Hercules soaked her feet in brine and vinegar for three weeks before a 1928 Madison Square Garden marathon. So successful was the method that when the New York health commissioner finally ended the dance, after three weeks, Mary was still feeling no pain.

Starting pistol ready, a promoter prepares to launch a marathon in Dallas. The tidiness of the contestants demonstrates that the event has not yet begun.

The Four-wheeled American Dream

"Why on earth do you need to study what's changing this country?" asked a lifelong resident and shrewd observer of the Middle West. "I can tell you what's happening in just four letters: A-U-T-O."
MIDDLETOWN BY ROBERT AND HELEN LYND, 1929

In the '20s the automobile created the greatest revolution in American life ever caused by a single device. It changed courtship habits and family ways, allowed more workers to live in green country and commute to city jobs and ended the farmer's dreary isolation. It decentralized cities and created huge, sprawling suburbs, took families off for Sunday outings and decreased church attendance. It gave hard-working Americans an escape to fun and new sights, reasserted their independence and saddled them with debt (by 1925, three of every four cars were bought on the installment plan).

It transformed the country's economy. With 23 million cars registered (in the late '20s), the automobile became America's biggest industry—its single largest customer for steel, lead, rubber, nickel and gasoline, as well as its most desired commodity. Rent and insurance excepted, one dollar of every five that consumers spent went for autos and their upkeep.

But the auto was more than a practical means; it struck roots deep in the national psyche, became part of the American dream. "To George F. Babbitt," wrote Sinclair Lewis in 1922, "as to most prosperous citizens of Zenith, his motor car was poetry and tragedy, love and heroism."

The manual laborer on the south side of the tracks felt the same way. Asked what the men were working for, a trade union official replied: "Twenty-five percent are fighting to keep their heads above water; 10% want to own their own homes; 65% are working to pay for cars." A working-class wife, interviewed by sociologists Robert and Helen Lynd for their book, *Middletown*, commented: "I'd rather go without food than give up the car."

Meanwhile, the object of this adoration grew even more desirable, acquiring hydraulic brakes in 1920, balloon tires in 1922. It became more attractive, with sweeping, rakish fenders and fast-drying colorful lacquers, and more comfortable, too. In 1919 some 90 per cent of auto bodies were open; 10 years later 90 per cent were closed. While the mass producers reached for new records (5.3 million cars in 1929), a few companies were providing the rich and near-rich with individuality and distinction. "In the city of Zenith," wrote Lewis, "a family's motor indicated its social rank and where Babbitt as a boy had aspired to the Presidency, his son Ted aspired to a Packard Twin Six."

It was the Golden Age of the automobile. Cars were never handsomer—and they were making changes in the way Americans lived; changes that would never be reversed.

Two for the Sports Set

It is usual for catalogues to deal in superlatives.

But the Stutz motor car has no need of superlatives. Allow us to say simply this:

"It is our conviction that this new Stutz is the greatest car ever built."

STUTZ BROCHURE

The Stutz Motor Car Company led a double life. It produced some of the most luxurious automobiles in the U.S.; it also built some of the world's toughest competition cars. Both types reflected a Stutz passion for technical excellence. The sporty custom-built Torpedo illustrated here had a long list of safety features including hydraulic brakes, all-round safety glass, and a "Noback" device that prevented the car from rolling back on hills ("the great army of women drivers, particularly, will welcome this innovation").

The Pierce-Arrow two-passenger runabout boasted a powerful six-cylinder dual-valve engine and a low-slung body that was not only an esthetic delight but a contribution to the car's roadability. ("Graceful lines," said the company's catalogue, "are as essential as adequate power.") This custom-built machine came equipped with a number of interesting extras, including a power-driven air pump for inflating the tires, an inspection lamp and a grease gun for do-it-yourself lubrication. It cost about $7,000.

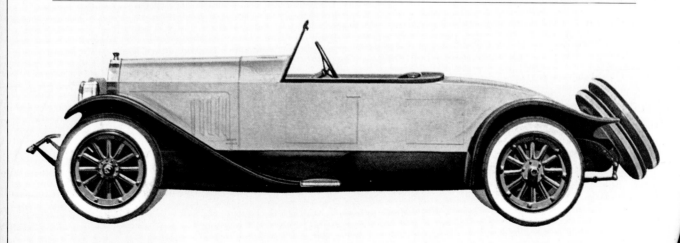

1921 Pierce-Arrow Two-Passenger Runabout

Picture Credits

The sources for the illustrations which appear in this book are shown here. Credits for the pictures from left to right are separated by semicolons, from top to bottom by dashes.

Cover—Nickolas Muray.

2,3—Culver Pictures. 5—Library of Congress. 6—UPI/Bettmann Newsphotos (2)—Underwood and Underwood/The Bettmann Archive; The Bettmann Archive. 7—State Historical Society of Wisconsin; Underwood and Underwood/The Bettmann Archive—Library of Congress; UPI/Bettmann Newsphotos. 9—Culver Pictures. 10,11—*Jazzmen*/Ramsey Archive. 12—Photo Files. 13—From *A Pictorial History of Jazz* by Orrin Keepnews and Bill Grauer Jr., Crown Publishers, 1966. 14—Edward Steichen, Collection The Museum of Modern Art, New York. 16,17—Wide World. 19—From *Life,* September 22, 1921, courtesy J. B. & R. Inc. 21—© The New York Times 1929. 22, 23—The New York Times. 25—The Bettmann Archive. 26—Culver Pictures; no credit—Culver Pictures; from *Life,* June 13, 1930, courtesy J. B. & R. Inc. 27—From *Life,* September 13, 1929, courtesy J. B. & R. Inc.; Sy Seidman—from *Life,* May 17, 1929, courtesy J. B. & R. Inc.; Culver Pictures. 29—Nickolas Muray. 30—Culver Pictures. 31—UPI/Bettmann Newsphotos. 32,33—Bert Morgan. 35—*The Detroit News.* 36—Underwood and Underwood/The Bettmann Archive; California Historical Society, San Francisco. 37—Museum of the City of New York; Courtesy Pabst Brewing Co. 38,39—Collection of Frank Rogers and Son. 41—From *Life,* October 4, 1929, courtesy J. B. & R. Inc. 42—From *Life,* June 28, 1929, courtesy J. B. & R. Inc.; from *Life,* April 26, 1929, courtesy J. B. & R. Inc.; from *Life,* May 10, 1929, courtesy J. B. & R. Inc.; from *Life,* September 6, 1929, courtesy J. B. & R. Inc. 43—From *Life,* July 19, 1929, courtesy J. B. & R. Inc.; from *Life,* July 12, 1929, courtesy J. B. & R. Inc.—from *Life,* June 21, 1929, courtesy J. B. & R. Inc.; from *Life,* August 30, 1929, courtesy J. B. & R. Inc. 45—Underwood and Underwood/The Bettmann Archive. 46,47—Culver Pictures (2). 48,49—Culver Pictures (4). 50—Culver Pictures except top right The Museum of Modern Art/Film Stills Archive. 51—Culver Pictures—The Bettmann Archive; The Museum of Modern Art/Film Stills Archive. 52,53—Culver Pictures except top left © 1988 Bubbles, France. 55—UPI/Bettmann Newsphotos. 56—Brown Brothers. 57—*The Baltimore Sun.* 58,59—UPI/Bettmann Newsphotos. 60,61—Collection of Frank Rogers and Son. 63—Henry Austin Clark Jr., The Long Island Automotive Museum, Glen Cove.